HEAVEN ON EARTH

Living as in the Kingdom of Heaven on Earth

REV. CONRAD C. HENRY SR.

ARPress
ILLUMINATING IDEAS
EMPOWERING VOICES

ARPress
45 Dan Road Suite 5
Canton MA 02021

Hotline: 1(888) 821-0229
Fax: 1(508) 545-7580

Ordering Information:
Quantity sales. Special discounts are available on quantity purchases by corporations, associations, and others. For details, contact the publisher at the address above.

Printed in the United States of America.

ISBN-13:	Softcover	979-8-89676-243-0
	eBook	979-8-89676-244-7

Library of Congress Control Number: 2025901206

HEAVEN
ON
EARTH

Living as in the Kingdom of
Heaven on Earth

Table of Contents

Chapter 1

HEAVEN ON EARTH

In the Kingdom of Heaven and Earth, there is only one God, and His name is Jehovah, Almighty God, Supreme God, the only True and Living God, there is no other gods beside Him. He is God and Father, Creator of Heaven and Earth and all that therein. Gen. 1. He is also the Redeemer of the lost soul of fallen men, through His Word, which He called His begotten Son. God called His Words His Son; For, In the beginning was the Word, and the Word was with God, and the Word was God. John 1:1; and Jesus said, I, and my Father are one. John 10:30. In the book of Matthew 1:23, Behold, a virgin shall be with child, and shall bring forth a son, and they shall call his name Emmanuel, which being interpreted is God with us. There are many other scriptures which clarifies, Jesus Christ, the Savior, and Redeemer, are one as God the Father and Creator.

God is also the Holy Spirit, and Administrator, Ambassador and Distributer of the gift of God in the Kingdom of heaven on earth. Gen. 1:2b; As Administrator, He supervise all the events of the creation. And the Spirit of God moved upon the face of the waters, so the Spirit of God was also very active in the Creation of the heaven and earth.

As Distributor, He gave spiritual gifts to men. Eph. 4:11,12; And he gave some apostles; and some, prophets; and some, evangelists: and some, pastors and teachers. For the perfecting of the saints, for the work of the ministry, for the edifying of the body of Christ (The Church). As Administrator, He oversees the gifts, that was distributed to the church. 1 Cor. 12:4-6, Now there are diversities (or differences) of gifts, but the same Spirit. And there are differences of administrations, but the same Lord. And there are diversities (or differences) of operations, but it is the same God which worketh all in all.

As Ambassador, he represented the King of heaven on earth. John 16:7-11; and Jesus said unto them. Nevertheless, I tell you the truth; it is expedient for you that I go away: for if I go not away, the Comforter will not come unto you; but if I depart, I will send him unto you. And when he is come, he will reprove (or convict) world of sin, and of righteousness, and of judgement. Of sin, because they believe not on me; Of righteousness, because I go to my Father, and ye see me no more: Of judgment, because the prince (Satan) of this world is judged. V.13: Howbeit when he, the Spirit of truth, is come, he will guide you into all truth: for he shall not speak of himself; but whatsoever he shall hear, that shall he speak: and he will shew you things to come.

The Holy Spirit came on the day of Pentecost. Acts 2:1-4: And when the day of Pentecost was fully come, they were all with one accord in one place. And suddenly there came a sound from heaven as of a rushing mighty wind, and it filled all the house where they were sitting. And there appeared unto them cloven tongues like as of fire, and it sat upon each of them. And they were all filled with the Holy Ghost, and began to speak with other tongues, as the Spirit gave them utterance. The Holy Spirit came as promise, and the disciples were filled as promise. There is no need to call for the Holy Spirit to come down from heaven now, He is already here. All three are one; God the Father, Jesus Christ the Son and the Holy Spirit; 1 John 5:7; For there are three bear record in heaven, the Father, the Word (Jesus Christ), and the Holy Ghost: these three are one. For there is One Lord, one faith, one baptism. One God and Father of all, who is above all, and through all, and in you all. Eph. 4:5-6; 1 John 5:8; And there are three that bear witness in earth, (The Kingdom of Heaven on Earth). The Spirit, and the Water, and the Blood: and these three agree in one. These three are necessary, for the conception of the new birth for life everlasting and never die, which is to be born again.

Chapter 2

THE CHURCH IS THE KINGDOM

The Church represents the Kingdom of Heaven on Earth, it is the greatest institution on earth, and the most powerful. It was founded by Jesus Christ, and he declares that the gates of hell shall not, cannot and will not prevail against it. The Kingdom of Heaven came to earth in the person, and the birth of Jesus Christ. Matt. 1:23 Behold, a virgin shall be with child, and shall bring forth a son, and they shall call his name Emmanuel, which being interpreted is, God with us. The Old Testament testified to it, Isaiah 7:14, Therefore the Lord himself shall give you a sign: a virgin shall conceive, and bear a son, and shall call his name Immanuel. God with us. Again, Isaiah evaluated him in chapter 9:6; For unto us a child is born, unto us a son is given: and the government shall be upon his shoulder: and his name shall be called Wonderful, Counsellor, The Mighty God, The Everlasting Father, The Prince of Peace. The book of Revelation recognized him as King of kings, and Lord of Lords. Rev. 19:16; And he hath on his vesture and on his thigh a name written, KING OF KINGS, AND LORD OF LORDS. The Church is to uphold the characteristic of the Kingdom of Heaven on earth as it is in Heaven in Holiness and Righteousness, to demonstrate the Love of God on earth, and the Truth of God in the earth; also, to show the way to the Kingdom of God, and to worship Him in Spirit and Truth.

The kingdom of God must be proclaimed by the Local church's consistently without any wavering of the message, throughout the world, there is no place in the church for compromising or toleration of sin, but must fight against it vehemently.

John the Baptist, forerunner to Jesus, instructed his listeners to Repent for the Kingdom of heaven is at hand. Matt. 3:2; Jesus certified it, when he began his preaching, Matt. 4:17; From that time Jesus began to preach, and to say, Repent, for the Kingdom of Heaven is at hand.

The disciples were instructed to enforce it by Jesus Christ, Matt. 10:7; And as ye go, preach, saying the Kingdom of Heaven is at hand.

Daniel has a forecast of the kingdom, and wrote about the power of the kingdom. And there was given him dominion, and glory, and a kingdom, that all people, nations, and languages, should serve him: his dominion is and everlasting dominion, that which shall not be destroyed. Daniel 7:14.

The kingdom of heaven on earth is spiritual, and cannot be seen with the human eyes, or be entered by a physical man. Even though some may believe that there are other ways to get into the Kingdom of Heaven on earth.

There is only one way.

Jn. 3:3; Jesus answered and said unto him, verily, verily, I say unto thee, except a man be born again, he cannot see the kingdom of heaven; again, in Jn. 3:5; Jesus, answered, verily, verily, I say unto thee, except a man be born of water and of the spirit, he cannot enter into the kingdom of God. That which is born of flesh is flesh, and that which is born of the spirit is spirit. Marvel not that I say unto thee, ye must be born again. There is no other way, but by spiritual birth. If you have not received the new birth, you are not in the kingdom of Heaven.

Chapter 3

KINGDOM PRAYER

Jesus instructed us that we should pray like we are already in the kingdom, for after this manner we should include in our prayer. Our Father which art in heaven, Hollowed be thy name. Thy kingdom come; Thy will be done in earth, as it is (carrying on) in heaven, so shall it be also be carrying on in earth.

Thy Will be done on earth, as it is in heaven. The Will of God in the kingdom of heaven in heaven, is that He is the only true and living God, the Creator and Sustainer of all, and there is no God before Him, or with him. And the same should be demonstrate in the Kingdom of Heaven on earth, and proclaimed throughout the whole world, to be acknowledged by every man, beast of the field, birds in the air, and fishes in the sea, that there is only one true and living God, and there is no other.

Exodus 20:2-5; I am the Lord thy God, which have brought thee out of the land of Egypt, out of the house of bondage.

Thou shalt have no other gods before me. (Exodus 20:23; Ye shall not make with me gods of silver, neither shall ye make unto you gods of gold.) Thou shalt not make unto thee any graven image, or any likeness of anything that is in heaven above, or that in the earth beneath, or that is in the water under the earth.

Thou shalt not bow down thyself to them, nor serve them: for I the Lord thy God am a jealous God. (Exodus 34:14. For thou shalt not worship no other god: for the Lord, whose name is Jealous, is a jealous God.)

So as the angels, and the host of heaven worship the Lord our God in heaven day and night, so shall we on earth should worshipped Him day and night. For there is no other God besides Him.

On earth as it is in heaven, the kingdom of heaven on earth, the will of God must be carried out, and by all being, weather in heaven or on earth must acknowledge Jesus Christ as the Son of God. And he is truly from God the father and creator of all things. Jn. 1:1,2; In the beginning was the Word, and the Word was with God, and the Word was God. The same was in the beginning with God.

Again; Jesus Christ, is the spoken Word of God which was spoken in the beginning, and God said let there be, and there it was, it was the Word, the begotten Son of God, Jesus Christ, performed all the work of creation.

Chapter 4

KING OF THE KINGDOM

In the kingdom of heaven on earth, there is only one king, and his name is Jesus Christ. (King of kings) Phil. 2:9-11; Wherefore God also hath highly exalted him, and given him a name which is above every name: That at the name of Jesus every knee should bow, of things in earth, and things under the earth; And that every tongue should confess that Jesus Christ is Lord, to the glory of God the Father.

It is also written in the scriptures of Him: Psalms 95:6; O come, let us worship and bow down: let us kneel before the Lord our maker.

Isaiah 45:23; I have sworn by myself, the word is gone out of my mouth in righteousness, and shall not return, That, unto me every knee shall bow, every tongue shall swear.

Matt. 28:18; And Jesus came and spake unto them, (his disciples) saying. All power is given unto me in heaven and in earth. The acknowledgement of Jesus Christ as the Son of the Living God, and that He is from God is the only way into the kingdom of heaven. He clarifies it in John 14:6; Jesus saith unto him, I am the way, the truth, and the life: no man cometh unto the Father, but by me.

The fact is, nothing, or by any other means can get you into the kingdom of heaven, but through Jesus Christ. No money, you cannot buy your way in, no rituals or traditions can get you in, no Virgin Mary can get you in, even though she should be honored for keeping herself pure, to be chosen, and to bare the Son of God, but she should not be worship. You cannot enter, because you attend a church, or being baptize, or speak in tongues, until you bow your knees, and repent of your sins, you will not enter into the kingdom of heaven on earth or in heaven. There are those that say that when one dies in Christ, they immediately goes to heaven, and that is far from the truth; but when one dies in the Lord, they immediately goes into the kingdom of heaven on earth, and it is a spiritual dimension, awaits the return of Jesus, who promise that he will return and receives us unto himself. Acts 1:10-11; And while they looked steadfastly toward heaven as he went up, behold, two men stood by them in white apparel: Which also said, ye men of Galilee, why stand ye gazing up into heaven? This same Jesus, which is taken up into heaven, shall come in like manner as ye have seen him go into heaven. He is coming back.

Chapter 5

KINGDOM CITIZENSHIP

The only way of citizenship in the Kingdom of Heaven is through Spiritual Birth, Ye must be born again, not by works of righteousness lest any man should boast. There is no strangers or foreigners in the Kingdom, only citizen. Ephesians 2:12 & 19;

V.12; That at that time ye were without Christ, being aliens from the commonwealth of Israel, and strangers from the covenants of promise, having no hope, and without God in the world.

V.19; Now therefore ye are no more strangers and foreigners, but fellow citizens with the saints, and of the household of God. There is no foreigners, aliens, or strangers in the kingdom of heaven, but all born again certified citizen.

There is only one understanding of languages in the kingdom of the word of God, even though there are many tongues, it does not matter of which country your originally from. With the coming of the Holy Ghost, God confounded those men who were from country and speak different languages. (Read) Acts 2:1-12; Verses 8; And how hear we every man in our own tongue, wherewith we were born.

Chapter 6

FLAG OF THE KINGDOM

Every Kingdom has a Flag, and the Flag for the Kingdom of heaven on earth is the Cross: The Cross is the flag of the kingdom that symbolizes the undying Love of God towards mankind. The Cross declares Victory. Upon the Cross, the ultimate sacrifice has been made and offered up to God for the sins of men. (It is Finish); complete, no more sacrifice needed to be offered up, such as; bulls and rams or any other sacrifices will be able to atoned for the sins of men. The birth of the church was delivered on the cross, just as Adam gave birth to the woman, for the woman was taken out of him; Gen. 2:21-22; Jesus death on the cross gives birth to everyone that put their trust in him, by water and Spirit (blood), John 3:5; Jesus answered, Verily, verily, I say unto thee, Except a man be born of water and of the Spirit, he cannot enter into the kingdom of God. Upon the cross, when the soldier pierced his side with his sword, water and blood came out of Him; which is the same procedure a woman must encounter giving birth to a child, water and blood. John 19:34; But one of the soldiers with a spear pieced his side, and forthwith came there out blood and water.

1 John 5:6; This is he that came by water and blood, even Jesus Christ; not by water only, but by water and blood. And it is the Spirit that beareth witness, because the Spirit is truth.

The Cross is the Flag that every born-again Christian should wave and lifted high, it identifies their citizenship of the King of Heaven on Earth. And I, if I be lifted up from the earth, will draw all men unto me. Jn. 12:32; the Christian flag should not be just recognized as a piece of cloth or metal with a symbol on it, but should Spiritualized and Visualizing the pain and the agony that our Lord and Savior suffer for the sins of this world, (For all have sinned, and come short of the glory of God. Rom 3:23). On the Cross he demonstrated His Love to all mankind. Without the cross, there is no resurrection, and without the resurrection, there is no salvation. The pledge of allegiance to the Cross which is the Flag of the kingdom of heaven on earth, can also be written as: I pledge allegiance to the Cross, which is the Christian Flag, and to the Savior for whose Kingdom it stands in heaven and earth: One Lord and Savior, Crucified, Risen and are coming again, with all his Saints, with everlasting life and freedom forever for all that put their trust in him. Amen

Chapter 7

THE CONSTITUTION OF THE KINGDOM OF HEAVEN

Hear, O Israel, and the rest of the world: The Lord our God is one: Lord. Deut. 6:4; And thou shalt love the Lord thy God with all thy heart, and with all thy soul, and with all thy mind, and with all thy strength, and Him only shall thou worship, and Thou shalt love thy neighbor as thy self. Mark 12:30,31; For God so loved the world, that he gave his only begotten Son, that whosoever (all men, male and female) believeth in him should not perish, but have everlasting life. For God sent not his Son into the world to condemn the world; but that the world through him might be saved. When Christ cries out on the cross father forgive them, for they know not what they do. The sins of the whole world were forgiven, every man's sin, from Adam up to the crucifiers on that day, but only those that accepted His forgiveness were forgiven and pardon even from the grave. He that believeth on him is not condemned: but he that believeth not is condemned already, because he hath not believed in the name of the only begotten Son of God. John 3:16-18; But God commended (show His great Love) toward us, in that, while we (the people) were yet sinners, Christ died for us. Rom. 5:8. There is therefore now no condemnation to them which are in Christ Jesus, who walk not after the flesh, but after the flesh. Rom 8:1. And be ye kind one to another, tenderhearted, forgiving one another, even as God for Christ's sake hath forgiven you. Eph. 4:3

Chapter 8

A JUDICIAL SYSTEM SETUP IN THE KINGDOM

In the kingdom of heaven on earth: there is a judicial system that has been setup in the kingdom for the citizen of the kingdom, so that those that have their differences can settle it in the kingdom with each other without going to the secular courthouse systems, before canal judges and magistrates. To the best of my knowledge, I have not heard of any churches that adapt this system or teaches it to its congregations, but I maybe wrong and I stand to be corrected. The church which is the kingdom of God has the authority and power to setup this system in the body of the church; believers have the right to report their grievances to the church, which then setup a board of elders or deacons, who will judge the matter without partiality to anyone, and judge the matters with all spiritual fairness. This board of Elders or Deacons must be God fearing, without compromising, and Holy Ghost fill. This board is only used when both parties cannot settle the matter between themselves. The necessary steps must be taken before the board can participate in the matter. Let's hear what our Lord Jesus Christ of the Kingdom has to say about it, for he instituted this system. Matt. 18:15-18; Moreover, if thy brother shall trespass against thee, go and tell him his fault between thee and him alone: if he shall hear thee, thou hast gained thy brother. V16; But if he will not hear thee, then take with thee one or two more, that in the mouth of two or three witnesses every word may be established. V17; And if he shall neglect to hear them, tell it to the church. (board): but if neglect to hear the church, let him be unto thee as a heathen man and a publican. The church has the power and authority to excommunicate or no longer have fellowship with any member who refuses to adhere too, or accept the decision of the church until they repented of their sin.

It is detrimental to settle your differences with your brother before you even pray; hear the words of our Lord and Savior. Matt. 5:23-24; Therefore, if thou bring thy gift to the alter, and there remember that thy brother hath ought against thee: V.24; Leave there thy gift before the alter, and go thy way: first reconciled to thy brother, and then come and offer thy gift. Can anyone of us that can testified that we have done this, if so, God be praise!

We have used Matt. 7:1-2: as an escape route, so that we don't have to give a verdict base on the evidence presented to us; so we quote Matt. 7:1-2; The bible say that we shouldn't judge, but we only read the first verse; Judge not, lest ye be judged. But the second verse details it; For with what judgement ye judge, ye shall be judged, by the master. If when you judge others you judge partially, unfairly, hatefully, despiteful, etc. etc., when you are judge by others in the same manner don't complain. The final analyst of all decisions should end with Love and Forgiveness from both believers in Christ. There is a disciplinary system also setup in the kingdom of chastisement in the kingdom of heaven, but there is no condemnation in the kingdom, chastisement while you are living here on earth and are subject to do something foolish in the flesh, God will chastise you, so to gain your attention that you are his child and must be corrected of your error, for whom the Lord loves He chasteneth, and scourgeth every son whom he receiveth. (Heb. 12:6), but there is no condemnation in the kingdom of heaven for you are eternally saved. Rom. 8:1; There is therefore now no condemnation to the which are in Christ Jesus, who walk not after the flesh, but after the spirit.

Judicial Support: 1 Corinthians 6:1 thru 6.

Chapter 9

NATIONAL ANTHEMS FOR THE KINGDOM

Every Nation has a National Anthem, and many Spiritual songs can be chosen as a national anthem for the Kingdom of Heaven on Earth such as; Amazing Grace; Jesus Keep me near the Cross; All Hail the Power of Jesus Name; Crown Him with Many Crowns; The Old Rugged Cross.

Just about every Christian Hymns are a contribution to the Cross, and its too many to single out any specific one for everybody likeness. A page will be left intentionally for you to write any one of your favorite hymn or hymns, that will contribute to the National Anthem of the Kingdom of Heaven on earth.

Here is one of my favorites:

Vs.1 When I survey the wondrous cross. On which the Prince of Glory died, my richest gain I count but loss, and pour contempt on all my pride.

Vs.2. Forbid it, Lord that I should boast, Save in the death of Christ my God. All the vain things that charm me most I sacrifice them to His blood.

Vs.3. See, from His head, His hand, His feet. Sorrow and love flow mingled down. Did e'er such love and sorrow meet, or Thorns compose so rich a crown?

INTENTIONALLY LEFT BLANK:

YOU MAY SELECT YOUR OWN PERSONAL KINGDOM ANTHEM;

Chapter 10

THE KINGDOM OF HEAVEN

The Kingdom of Heaven is one in two locations, in heaven and on earth. (1) In Heaven where the Throne of God the Father and Creator, The Great I AM; the only True and Living God, (Our Father who art in heaven) and where Jesus Christ, Our Lord, Saviour and Redeemer, are daily making intercession for all who trusted in Him. (Rom. 8:27 And he that searcheth the hearts knoweth what is the mind of the Spirit, because he maketh intercession for the saints according to the will of God.) Again, Who is he that condemneth? It is Christ that died, yea rather, that is risen again, who is even at the right hand of God, who also maketh intercession for us. And (2) on earth, Thy Kingdom come on earth, so, the Kingdom of God is on earth, where the Holy Spirit is the Administrator, and where all born again Christians home is, until He come again. For Jesus Christ said John 14:1-3 Let not your heart be troubled: ye believe in God, believe also in me. In my Father's house are many mansions: if it were not so, I would have told you. I go to prepare a place for you. And if I go and prepare a place for you, I will come again, and receive you unto myself; that where I am, there ye may be also. Jesus knew his time to leave this world was coming to an end, and did not want his disciples to feel abandon, neglected and no provision was made them and their services, in Jn. 14:18: Jesus assured them again, I will not leave you comfortless, I will come again.

No born again Christians, when they die goes into the Kingdom of heaven in heaven, but goes into the kingdom of heaven on earth, patiently awaits the return of our Lord and Saviour as he had promise. It's a fault's hope promise to you by some of our preachers, and not by Jesus, how can you go to heaven when you die, when Jesus say: I'll come again and received you unto myself. The apostle Paul wrote to the church in 1 Thessalonians 4:16-18; about the coming of the Lord; For the Lord himself shall descend from heaven with a shout, with the voice of the archangel, and with the trump of God: and the dead in Christ shall rise first: V.17; Then we which are alive and remain shall be caught up together with them in the clouds, to meet the Lord in the air: and so shall we ever be with the Lord. V.18; Wherefore comfort one another with these words. Yes, Christ will return for all who believes and put their trust in him: He will triumphantly return to receive all born again believers. For, in a moment, in the twinkling of an eye, at the last trump: for the trumpet shall sound, and the dead shall be raised incorruptible, and we shall be change. 1 Cor. 15:52. Those of us who have love ones, who had gone on before us can comfort ourselves that they are in a good place, and they are safe and in good hands, resting from their labor.

Chapter 11

THE KINGDOMS COME TOGETHER

When all thing is accomplish, such as the return of Jesus for his saints, the Rapture, the war of ARMAGEDDON, the seven Plagues, the Anti-christ is identified, the mark of the beast in full force upon those that receives his mark and worship him, and every event that was prophesied to happen before the world end, Satan, the Devil, which was bound for a thousand years will be loose for a little season and shall deceived many, and every man stand before God at the great white throne judgement to received their fate of their final destination.

Revelation 20:12-15; And I saw the dead, small and great (good and bad) stand before God (The Supreme and Righteous Judge); and the books were opened (The books of works), and another book was opened (The registry of the new birth) which is the book of life: and the dead were judged out of those things which were written in the books (Every works that one has committed in their lifetime will be judge by their works, but will not be saved by their works. For by Grace ye are saved, and not of works) And the sea gave up the dead which were in it; and death and hell delivered up the dead which were in them: (Those that were hold captive by death and hell, release to stand and represent themselves before the judgement seat of God for themselves, no one will be accountable for another actions, but everyone must stand up and gives account for themselves). There is no plea bargain, delay, or appeals, when those books are open that's it, all your works will be exposed whether good or evil. Now when the book is open, which is the book of life, and the roll calls of names is called, and your name is not written in the book of life which is your new name that was given to everyone at their new birth, (Ye must be born again) and was written in the book of life it's the only way to eternal life. Rev. 20:15; And whosoever was not found written in the book of life was cast into the lake of fire.

It has been said, let the work I've done speak for me, but when the books were opened, which is the books that contain all the works you have done in your life time as you stand before the Righteous Judge on judgement day, all your works will be credited to you; whether good or evil, but it will not be accounted for your salvation. For it is; Not by works of righteousness which we have done, but according to his mercy he saved us, by the regeneration, and renewing of the Holy Ghost. (Titus 3:5) Some will even declare that they done marvelous works; Matt. 7:22-23; Many will say to me in that day, Lord, Lord, have we not prophesied in thy name? and in thy name cast out devils? And in thy name done many wonderful works? Here is the surprise; And then will profess unto them, I never knew you: depart from me, ye that work iniquity. Yes, there are many who have done some very good works, yet they are not saved, because they rejected the only begotten Son of God, who gave his life on the cross as a living sacrifice for the salvation of fallen mankind, they refused to repent of their sins, and accepted Jesus Christ as their Lord and Saviour; but rely on their good works. For your name to be written in the book of life, you must be born again, and the only way to be born again, you must acknowledge your are a sinner, and you need a Saviour, repent of your sins, ask for forgiveness, baptizes, and accept Jesus Christ as your Lord and Saviour in your life, then will you receive the new birth, new name and your name written in the book of life; remember you cannot work to be saved, but you are saved to do good works.

Chapter 12

NEW LIFE ENJOYED

Revelation 21:1; And I saw a new heaven and a new earth: for the first heaven and the first earth were passed away: and there was no more sea. And I John saw the holy city, new Jerusalem, coming down from God out of heaven, prepared as a bride adorned for her husband. And I heard a great voice out heaven saying, Behold, the tabernacle of God is with men, and He (God) will dwell with them, and they shall be his people, and God himself shall be with them, and their God. I am very excited about being in the present of God in the new Jerusalem, worshiping every day. And God shall wipe away all tears from their eye; and there shall be no more death, neither sorrow, nor crying, neither shall there be any more pain: for the former things are passed away. Praises the Lord. When we all get to heaven, the new Jerusalem, what a day of rejoicing that will be, forever, and forever. Amen. TO GOD BE THE GLORY.

www.ingramcontent.com/pod-product-compliance
Lightning Source LLC
Chambersburg PA
CBHW051253120626
46547CB00014B/1925